Designing Teacher Study Groups
A Guide for Success

Designing Teacher Study Groups
A Guide for Success

Emily Cayuso
Carrie Fegan
Darlene McAlister

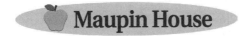

Designing Teacher Study Groups:
A Guide for Success

Book Design: Katrina Vitkus
Cover Design: Gaye Dell

Library of Congress Cataloging-in-Publication Data

Cayuso, Emily, 1954-
Designing teacher study groups : a guide for success / Emily Cayuso,
Carrie Fegan, Darlene McAlister.
    p. cm.
Includes bibliographical references.
ISBN 0-929895-68-1 (pbk.)
1. Teacher work groups—United States. 2. Teachers—In-service
training—United States. 3. Book clubs (Discussion groups)—United
States. I. Fegan, Carrie, 1973- II. McAlister, Darlene, 1957- III.
Title.
LB1731.C38 2004
370'.71'5—dc22

2003027761

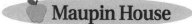

Maupin House Publishing, Inc.
PO Box 90148
Gainesville, FL 32607
1-800-524-0634 / 352-373-5588
352-373-5546 (fax)
www.maupinhouse.com
info@maupinhouse.com

*Publishing Professional Resources
that Improve Classroom Performance*

Table of Contents

Introduction

Our Story

In January, 2002 I approached my principal about my desire to start a study group at school. I had been feeling frustrated because many of the in-services offered for staff development, although good, were not appropriate for my needs as a reading specialist on campus. After hearing the same concerns expressed by my colleagues, I thought, *Wouldn't it be great if, as teachers, we could have more ownership of what we learn?* I met with my principal and pitched my plan: offer teachers a variety of literacy-related professional books to vote on, buy the book for the teachers with school funds, and for every hour the study group met give teachers time toward school district professional development hours. My principal was extremely supportive (a definite plus) and allowed me time to speak at the first faculty meeting after the Christmas break.

I told the faculty that even though I could not promise the Oprah Book Club, I would try my best to make the study group a fun learning experience. Like members of Oprah's Book Club, we would all be able to make text-to-self connections as teachers with whatever book was selected. After a one-week period, over which we voted on approximately fifteen book titles, ten teachers selected the skinniest book (that's exactly what they told me, "skinny").

We placed a rush on the book order, and in the days that followed, I set up ground rules, divided up the chapters for six meetings, and met briefly with the group to pass out the books and talk about expectations. I would facilitate the meetings and provide questions based on the readings to guide our conversation. We decided to meet once every two weeks during February, March, and April. The conference room at school was the most convenient location, so the group decided to meet there. A sign-up sheet was passed around for snacks. Thus, the first Will Rogers Elementary Study Group was born.

On the day of the first meeting I waited with nervous anticipation. The conference room was set up, snacks assembled, questions written on the dry-erase board, sticky notes, highlighters, and other note-taking supplies put out, and a sign-in sheet ready. I couldn't have predicted what happened next. Everyone arrived (on time) with their copies of Marcia Freeman's *Teaching the Youngest Writers: A Practical Guide* (the "skinny" book). *All* had completed the readings, and they began exchanging positive, enthusiastic comments even before the meeting began.

Needless to say, my nervousness was unfounded. There

was so much "book talk" going on that the group seemed to facilitate itself. "Skinny" turned out to be sensational, and teacher engagement was at its maximum. We were having so much fun other staff members were peering through the window, wanting to share in the excitement (or maybe just some food).

I thought after such a successful first meeting we might have already reached our peak, but I was wrong. The study group meetings continued to improve. Teachers came with more and more comments to share. We had "show and tell" each time; we shared writing samples (as per Marcia Freeman's lessons), ideas on classroom management, and writer's workshop lesson ideas. Each of us also started making a picture file and collecting other materials necessary to incorporate what we learned during study group into our daily classroom routines. Everyone shared spontaneously, freely exchanging personal reactions, questions, and ideas. We came to the meetings willingly, positively, and with plenty of appetite for the great variety of snacks and beverages each meeting offered.

Birth of the Book

We had made it halfway through *Teaching the Youngest Writers* when I received in my mailbox at school a flyer advertising a day long in-service with Marcia Freeman. How perfect! Oprah couldn't have planned this any better. Since my principal had been witnessing firsthand the success of the study group, it was not hard to persuade her to find funds to send four of the members of the group to spend a day with Marcia. Needless to say, of the group to spend a day with Marcia. Needless to say, we were pretty excited when we arrived that fateful day. Before the in-service began we introduced ourselves to Marcia and shared with her our tale of how the "skinny" book won out over all the others and how much we were enjoying our study group. Meeting Mrs. Freeman was delightful. Not only did she validate the connections we were making with her book, but almost immediately stated that we needed to share the wealth, and write a book about study groups. She would help. We thought, *You've got to be kidding. Impossible. No way.* Yet the more we talked—that day, back at school with the rest of the group, and later, through numerous e-mails—the more apparent it became that we had something to say.

Study groups are powerful vehicles for learning. Where else can you expand your knowledge base and understanding in a relaxed, social environment? Because each member of the group shares his/her own understanding of the text, study groups are highly interactive. All members can learn from the multiple points of view exchanged. Since the group takes a proactive approach toward learning I can honestly say they are fun. Can you say that about all in-services you've attended?

It is with all this in mind that we have designed this "skinny" book. We hope that, by providing you a framework and practical tips for a variety of study groups, our book will encourage you to start your own. May you have as much enjoyment, camaraderie, and success as we did. Have fun!

Emily Cayuso

1

What Are Teacher Study Groups?

"The professional study groups that we started at Edison serve to guide the teachers into doing more research that pertains to their subject areas. They also serve to teach the teachers the 'why' behind some of the requirements we place on them."

Dottie Uribe

Campus Instructional Coordinator

Before we begin this discussion, perhaps we should take a quick pre-test to assess your background knowledge.

What is a study group?

a) A gaggle of stressed out gabby girls and guys who meet to eat, drink, and be merry?

b) A mandated provision of education code 361.198765490 199?

c) A group of people who meet regularly to ex change ideas and knowledge about texts and/or other resources they are reading?

If your answer was "C," congratulations! You are right! Carlene Murphy, Director of Staff Development at Richmond County Public Schools, defines a study group as "a small number of individuals joining together to increase their capacities through new learning for the benefit of students." To elaborate further, study groups are quickly becoming a dynamic way for teachers to grow through teacher-created professional development.

As a member of a study group, an individual can seek and suggest clarification and interpretation of text or ideas, reinforce his or her own learning, receive encouragement, and develop a sense of belonging to a community of learners—facets of learning often missing when a person studies alone. Collaborating with other professionals is especially important for teachers and is a significant benefit of study groups. Study groups offer participants not mandated workshops, but rather the luxury of *choice* in terms of studying what interests the group.

Types of Study Groups

Study groups come in all shapes and sizes. A fancy definition would tell you that the word "study" suggests the activities of the group will include presentations and discussions of important new trends and developments in research or practice related to the topic under consideration. In other words, "anything goes." Study groups can serve many purposes. All center on the study of professional material. To meet your own group's specific needs, we suggest integrating useful aspects from a variety of study group models. The following is a list of our favorites.

Topic Study Groups (The Private Eye Method)

If a good mystery keeps you hanging on the edge of your seat, this is the group for you. Break out the magnifying glass, deerstalker hat, overcoat, pipe, and don a big moustache…uh, well, O.K. All you'll really need is a group of enthusiastic teachers, a room to gather in, notebooks, pens, highlighters, and some titillating texts. In a Topic Study Group, the members choose an area of focus based on their own needs assessment and then research available information on the topic. A staff member can suggest several choices of texts, articles, or video series for the group to investigate, and then solicit interested participants to choose which are most appealing. The group may then review and select from these materials.

In *What Really Matters for Struggling Readers*, Richard Allington (2001) refers to this type of study group as a TAPER (Teachers as Professional Education Readers) study group. The goal of a TAPER Study Group "…is to develop individual expertness and foster the development of shared knowledge among members of the group" (p.113). Each time the study group reconvenes, group members share their insights, seek clarification on ideas from the text, and make connections between the readings and their classrooms.

Our study group (see Introduction) was a Topic Study Group. We selected the book we wanted to read based on interest and need. We read through the book over a three-month time period, meeting every two weeks to share and discuss insights and knowledge gained.

Now, since the book we happened to be studying had lots of ideas on how to teach writing, some in the group took the initiative and tried out these ideas in their classes. This is not part of a Topic Study Group, but who's going to stop the creative juices from flowing? With that in mind, if you are seeking more "hands on" participation, more "show and tell," and a chance to hone your teaching skills, then the next type of group would be just right for you.

Practices Study Group (The Dr. Phil Study Group)

If you are into self improvement and New Age intro-spection, you would probably "dig" the Practices Study Group. Dr. Phil's often-asked question, "How's that working for you?" would certainly be helpful as teachers reflect in an introspective manner about their own teaching and how to improve it.

The Practices Study Group is designed to be a metacognitive learning tool. Members focus on a strat-egy that they learn and experiment with through active participation. Components of a Practices Study Group might include teachers watching videotapes of them-selves or others teaching, observing in other classrooms, or discussion within the group about ways to improve lesson presentation, classroom management, instruc-tional implementation, questioning practices, student learning styles, or pacing and movement through the lesson cycle.

Practices Study Groups might also involve the study of professional books, articles, or videotapes (as in a Topic

Study Group), but with the added expectation of "home-work." In other words, between scheduled meetings teachers will try out the lesson ideas, strategies, or concepts in their own classrooms. When the group reconvenes they can do several things:

- Share how the lesson and/or strategy they tried worked.

- Bring in work samples and/or products from the lesson for "show and tell."

- Share a videotape of themselves teaching the lesson or using the strategy in order to debrief and solicit feedback.

- Give a "mini teach" to the rest of the group on some aspect of the study group readings.

Alison Bapst, an educator in Sarasota, Florida, has conducted several successful Practices Study Groups with teachers across grade levels as well as within the same grade level at her school. One such group used Marcia Freeman's K-5 school-wide video series. Part of the meeting time was devoted to viewing and discussing the videos. As the facilitator, Ms. Bapst supplied ex-amples of student work and relevant children's litera-ture, as well as writing chart tablets that complemented the assigned reading for that week. During study group meetings, she would model a lesson from the reading to give teachers an idea of how the lessons would evolve. Group members also presented lessons they had tried and examples of resulting student work.

TIP Study Group

Richard Allington puts a new spin on Practices Study Groups with a study group called TIP (Teacher Inquiry Projects). Rather than rely on a determined set of resources, participants do their own research. The main focus of a TIP group is for the participants to gather as many resources and data as possible about a particular topic. These materials are researched and evaluated to determine their possible effectiveness in individual classrooms.

For example, if a group is wondering how to provide more effective ways of making conferencing a powerful teaching tool during writer's workshop, the group can research that topic. Possible resources might include books, articles in professional journals, and conversations with experts in the field. Group members probing for written information on the topic may decide to do their own investigation by observing other classrooms, taking surveys, talking with other teachers, or implementing in their own classrooms ideas gleaned from previous meetings. The International Reading Association refers to this type of study group as Teacher Research. Carol Lyons and Gay Su Pinnell, the authors of *Systems for Change in Literacy Education* (2001), identify this type of study group as an Action Research group.

Whether you call it a TIP group, or a Teacher or Action Research Group, Practices Study Groups lend themselves to real life classroom experiences and allow immediate reflection and in-depth discussion about teaching experiences. They offer unique opportunities for teachers to improve their teaching by listening to feedback from other professionals and ultimately using what they've learned to become their own critics.

Online Study Groups (Internet Café)

Are you bogged down with paper? Is it too difficult to arrange meetings with your group due to location or scheduling? Do you want to broaden the boundaries of your study group to include professionals from all over the country? If you answered yes to any of the above questions, then online study groups may be just the thing for you.

A great number of study groups currently operate online. Joining is as simple as logging on to Google (or any other search engine), typing in "study groups" and a specific topic or area of interest, and then scrolling the results for a desired or interesting feature. Established online study groups generally have a facilitator (more about the role of the facilitator in chapter 5), and the steps for joining are usually in place—and at the tips of your fingers.

The study group will commonly meet over a pre-determined period of time. Each week a different topic is discussed on the related issue or book. The facilitator maintains a discussion board where the participants may ask questions, share their progress, and read how other participants handle similar situations. As in all cases, it is also important to understand that just reading the material is not enough to produce results. Participants must be committed to applying what they have learned if they want to reap the benefits. It is also important to note that sometimes online study groups charge fees for their services. The drawback of Online Study Groups is that, without face-to-face interaction, camaraderie may be harder to attain. Plus, your friends won't be able to bring scrumptious treats to your meeting table. (See Great Study Group Munchies in chapter 8.)

You might also consider starting your own online study group. A user-friendly and cost-effective way of doing this would be to create a message board online or to use e-mail software to manage your group. If you are not computer savvy, you may want to contact your technology specialist on campus or your district technology department. The following websites offer software which may be helpful in managing an e-mail study group.

CMail List Server   http://www.computalynx.co.uk

LISTSERV for Windows/95

http://www.lsoft.com

MacJorDomo

www.macjordomo.med.cornell.edu/index.html

www.commtechlab.msu.edu/sites/letsnet/ noframes/bigideas/

Remember, this is just a sampling of study group types to choose from. Feel free to select bits and pieces from the different study group types discussed above and add them to your own ideas to make a group that is most practical for you and your group members.

2

Study Group Mania: Why Study Groups are Popular

"For me, our study group was a very relevant and hands-on form of professional development which we tailored to meet our own needs. Providing input into group discussions and voting on all aspects of topic study and group agenda gave me vested interest in what we were learning. I was able to apply what I'd learned immediately in the classroom and enjoyed learning about strategies which were effective in other classrooms, as well."

Ann Reagan
Kindergarten teacher

Empowered with Ownership

Let's put teachers in charge of their own learning. Good teaching stems from reflective thinking.

Research has demonstrated that student achievement increases when they are able to monitor their learning with metacognitive study strategies (Ormrod 2001). In effect, these students are learning how to be "in charge" of their own learning.

Acting as a facilitator, the teacher guides the students in taking ownership over their own cognitive development.

Teachers are learners, too. Study groups provide educators with the same opportunity to diagnostically critique various aspects of their own instruction in order to become more effective teachers.

These same factors have also been proven to be effective in the world of business. Consultants at Ownership Associates Incorporated report that research over the past 25 years shows employees are more productive when they have ownership in the company (*Ownership Culture Report*, 2001). Ownership can be defined in terms of a monetary incentive or a sense of belonging in the company. When asked what was most important to them, participating employees ranked fairness, participation in decision making, and sense of community or bond with other employees higher than they ranked monetary incentives and influencing company-wide policy.

The principles of ownership (being in charge) apply to teachers and staff development as well. Anne Jolly, an education program specialist for SERVE states, "Learning teams (referred to as 'study groups' in some schools) are the most effective, cost-efficient way for teachers to learn what changes are needed in their practice and then to make those changes. They also have the added benefit of building rapport, trust, and support" (Richardson, 2001). Thus, it may not be as effectual for school districts to mandate which type of professional development teachers should attend. Interestingly enough, an article published in the magazine *Reading Today* concurs: "The aim of IRA literacy study groups is to put teachers in charge of their own learning allowing them to play a larger role [in their own professional development]" (Farstrup, 2002, p. 8). A study group's flexibility presents the participants with the unique opportunity for ownership or control over what kind of study group they want to invest themselves in.

Let's Get Together, Yeah, Yeah, Yeah: Rapport, Collaboration, Cooperation, and Friendship

Study groups fill an important need, allowing colleagues to meet and to find wisdom and encouragement. The framework of a study group can satisfy each individual group member's personal needs while providing an arena for collaborating with other professionals vested with common interests. During the lifespan of a good study group, friendships are created and strengthened, and collegial bonds are built.

Have you ever finished a day of teaching and realized you were so engrossed in the activities in your own classroom that you had not spoken to another adult for more than two or three minutes at a time? We sometimes overlook the positive influence of relating to other teachers as professionals and friends. Since study groups provide life-enriching activities and lend themselves to creating collaborative learning, they not only benefit the individual, but can enhance school climate and staff morale as well.

During a staff development project called Partners in Science (see discussion below), teachers emphasized the "…need to have professional development that was relevant, ongoing, and long-term. The teachers felt that the most important need was time to work with their partner scientists and other teachers outside the classroom."

In *Trust in Schools: A Core Resource for Improvement,* University of Chicago professors Anthony S. Bryk and Barbara Schneider present data which link students' increased achievement with a school's trust levels. They feel that without "…a strong bond of trust among members of the school community…schools stand little chance of improving…" (as cited in Gewertz, October 16, 2002).

Bryk and Schneider state, "We view the need to develop relational trust as an essential complement both to governance efforts that focus on bringing new incentives to bear on improving practice and to instructional reforms that seek to deepen the technical capacities of school professionals."

Making it My Way: Meeting the Individual Needs of Teachers

Naturally the format of a study group is flexible. Its participants are put in the unique position of creating a study group that is based on their personal preferences. Group members can determine topics studied, group format, meeting agendas and dates, snacks, resources used, length of study, meeting location, assignments given, research explored, and ideas shared. (Variations on different group formats and getting your study group started are discussed more thoroughly in chapters 3, 4, and 5.) Study groups are created for teachers, by teachers.

Top corporations in America have made millions off of a simple concept: the customer is always right. Corporations fashion their products to meet their clients' specific needs. Millions of satisfied customers return for products and services when they feel they have gotten exactly what they wanted. In order to give teachers the most satisfaction and feelings of a "job well done," various aspects of the group can be molded around what the participants want and need to learn.

In her article "Listening to Teachers," Leslie Sears Gordon (2002) describes a staff development workshop implemented in the Fairbanks North Star Borough School District. The workshop, called Partners in Science, involves the collaboration of scientists, experts, and professionals from universities and industry as "partner professionals" with teachers and technology. When the workshop began to flounder, the designers turned to the teacher participants for help and concentrated on their needs. The teachers "…identified content support from professionals, collaboration time, learning communities, and best-practice exploration as the most crucial aspects of the professional development." The project was re-worked on the teachers' suggestions, and six years later, it continues to be successful.

Getting to the Meat of Things

(In-depth research on teaching and learning: It's time for teachers to become the students.)

Study groups provide teachers with a forum to expand their content knowledge, build upon and update their expertise, learn new teaching techniques, and adapt successful methods to better meet the needs of their students. Carlene Murphy is an independent consultant for the Whole-Faculty Study Group Process and a staff development specialist for ATLAS Communities. In the *Journal of Staff Developments* she states, "…Whole-Faculty Study Groups blend different staff development approaches into classroom experiences for students" (1999). She goes on to say that when members of these study groups "…come together and focus on student learning, the range of knowledge, resources, and experience they bring to the process are blended together for a more powerful impact on all of their students."

Since the 1970s, European businesses have been conducting study groups similar to "think tanks" in the fields of mathematics and science. Their aim is to solve problems which have "direct industrial importance" (European Study Group with Industry 2001-2002). They have found them to be a successful setting for interdisciplinary collaboration and analytical reasoning.

Study groups also meet all the characteristics of high quality professional development. They:

- Provide an opportunity to analyze a variety of student achievement data (informal observations, examples of student written work and projects, feedback from students, and test results) when considering the progression of individual and collective learning.

• Can utilize a logical long-term method of planning, related to the campus plan, taking campus goals and students'/teachers' individual needs into consideration.

• Reserve time for professional learning to occur in a meaningful way.

• Promote and validate teachers as leaders and experts in their field.

• Build upon and enhance teachers' knowledge and instructional abilities.

• Encourage lifelong inquiry and reflection.

• Provide for group and individual study.

• Adhere to the standards of good teaching and learning practices (including creating a nourishing atmosphere and encouraging adult learning).

• Use open lines of communication, information-sharing, and community-wide collaboration to create broad-based support of professional development.

• Can include diagnostic evaluation of staff development.

Study groups are a perfect way for teachers to become superior educators. As professionals, teachers should continuously strive to increase their knowledge and expertise to more effectively meet the needs of their students and enhance student success. A well-run study group is the perfect place for teachers to meet, greet, share ideas, and research educational texts and materials.

3

Getting Started

"I looked forward to meeting with the book club because of the enthusiasm demonstrated by all the teachers there. When they found an idea in the book that worked well with the students, it got me motivated to also try it in my classroom."

Lindy Rodriguez
Second grade teacher

Study Group Goal Setting

Study groups begin with goal setting. To decide which topic your study group should address, it is helpful to analyze the following factors on your campus: student needs, test scores, teacher interests, district mandates, and trends in education. Some questions you might want to ask are

1. What are our strengths? (as a grade level, campus, or individual)

2. What are our weaknesses/areas needing improvement? (This could be weaknesses

on student test data, in teaching, or knowledge of curriculum subject matter.)

3. What do we have questions/concerns about?

4. What would we like more information about?

5. What priorities do we have? (as a grade level, campus, or individual)

You can discuss these or other questions informally or formally. Have a goal-setting discussion with your grade level, vertical team, or at a faculty meeting. If you prefer, you can place a survey in staff boxes and then analyze the information provided to determine what your focus of study will be. IRA has a survey form in the book *Facilitator's Guide: IRA Literacy Study Groups*. This reproducible form is a very practical goal-setting tool. As your group analyzes teacher input, surveys, and test data, your goal or goals should soon emerge.

When we created our study group, we asked teachers which curricular area they felt needed the most improvement. Their answers were based on student work in class and standardized test scores. Group members were most enthusiastic about addressing a key area of weakness found school-wide: the writer's workshop. Group members were given the chance to examine a variety of professional texts focusing on writing. They decided which book would be the most "teacher friendly," offer practical applications in the classroom, and help boost the writing program in their specific grade levels.

Remember, study groups can complement traditional ways of meeting a predetermined need such as faculty meetings, online classes, workshops, or conferences given by experts in the field. They are indeed an effective professional development program.

Who Will Participate?

Ideally, participation in a study group should be an individual teacher's choice. Once your study group has chosen a topic, those teachers who want to join should naturally step forward. The freedom and ease of this type of set up allows for greater ownership of learning.

Yet in many school settings teachers are not given an option about joining a study group. Membership in a study group can be part of school or district mandates. If this is the case, then joining a study group can follow specific guidelines. For example, teachers can be assigned to a study group with other similar grade level or department members. Administration can place teachers in groups that target specific objectives for improving teacher performance. Small study groups can also be formed, limiting membership to one member from each grade level to encourage cross-curricular sharing. Participants can be grouped by primary vs. intermediate, paraprofessionals, special programs teachers, administration, and parent groups. The possibilities are endless.

How to Find Resources to Study

Once you have found the target topic for your study group, you need to find the "perfect" reading material. If you like hunting for bargains, finding appropriate resources can actually be a lot of fun.

An easy place to start searching is by asking the members of the group or district curriculum specialists (for example, early childhood development, reading, math, or technology) to brainstorm title recommendations. In *What Really Matters for Struggling Readers: Designing Research Based Programs* (2001), Richard Allington suggests contacting a local educational retailer for book title suggestions. In addition, he mentions that it might be helpful to "check out the professional book review columns in educational journals" and to "visit websites with professional book reviews." He recommends Web sites like read.com, reading.org, ncte.org, and idonline.org. We offer additional suggestions in chapter 7.

Allington also reminds study groups to browse online for further reviews. In particular, he highlights amazon.com and bn.com as sites which provide good analysis of educational books. Other professional resources can be found on ERIC, or even by visiting your local teacher bookstore. Also, don't forget the many available videotaped series on education and instruction.

Resources can be selected to meet a particular area of growth on a campus (see discussion above about choosing a topic) or simply because individual groups of teachers, parents, or administrators find them highly motivational and applicable to their field and/or needs. For example, a parent or PTA study group might be formed to study best parenting practices or how to help their children improve their study habits. Administrators might want to create a study group centering on a particular theme such as management models for schools or leadership styles.

Choosing texts and videos around a central theme can also be the basis for your group's study. For example, a group could be formed to increase teacher knowledge of children's literature. Your librarian could facilitate a group that studies

- current children's literature
- different genres of expository and narrative texts
- children's literature appropriate for different developmental levels
- how to write children's books
- making the reading/writing connection through the use of children's literature
- poetry
- multicultural literature
- improving the effectiveness of teacher read alouds
- books for readers theater
- using children's literature to teach specific information

Don't Forget the Fun

Regardless of the topics and resources your group settles on, make sure you don't leave out the "fun" (otherwise known as "incentives," "compensation," or even "necessities").

Let's face it. Even though we are adults, we still like to be rewarded for our efforts. Although the days of receiving gold stars and cookies have long since past, a hearty pat on the back for a job well done or a simple "Thank you!" is never unwelcome.

The question remains: How can you motivate your fellow staff members about study groups? Fortunately, there is an unlimited supply of motivational resources just waiting to be tapped.

Credit
One of the biggest "carrots" for most teachers is receiving state-recognized credit towards required professional development hours or credit towards trade-out work days. This kind of incentive needs to be planned out in advance. You will need to discuss this possibility with your administrator and district offices for approval. Remember to refer to the specialist teachers (for example, your reading specialist, guidance counselors, or instructional coordinators). They often have already built a rapport with the aforementioned personnel.

Ownership
Research shows people are more motivated and can comprehend information better when they feel they have ownership of, or have helped create, what they are learning about. It is important to give the teachers some say in the topic they will be studying. Allowing the participants to choose the topic will make the study group more relevant and can easily be done with a simple vote. A sense of ownership promotes immediate application in the classroom, and can be further fostered during group meetings by encouraging open discussion and by sharing practical applications and work samples generated by the group's readings.

Freebies

When the school purchases the materials the teachers have chosen to study, study groups become even more attractive. Ordering twelve books or a videotape series may be more cost-effective than sending several teachers to a three-day conference. And by purchasing the books for the participants the school is in effect saying, "We support and commend what you are doing. Great job! Keep up the good work."

Convenience

On-site staff development definitely has its advantages. Picture this: It's 3:05, all your students have left (fled) your classroom and their voices are fading down the hall. Your feet are sore, your back hurts, and you are tired and hungry. The last thing you want to do is rush out the door and drive 30 minutes to an obscure location for a lecture on some mandatory school district topic.

An on-site study group is a much more convenient and attractive option because you do not have to drive anywhere. That beautiful (and sometimes underused) conference room right down the hall will do. Imagine sitting in adult-sized chairs while interacting with highly educated and open-minded individuals who share common interests. Someone has signed up to bring snacks, everyone has read the pertinent material ahead of time, and some teachers have even brought along student work samples and ideas from their classroom to share.

No, it's not a dream. The above scenario is a description of a well-run study group.

Snacks

It goes without saying that if you feed them, they will come. So maybe we should have listed this first! Snacks are *very* important to teachers after a challenging day. By 3:30 p.m., the average teacher has made 5,000 decisions! Effective decision making and problem solving require a lot of brain power. Whatever you do, always have snacks. Savories, sweets, munchies, crunchies, pig-out favorites, and healthy treats—all are welcome.

Providing refreshments contributes to the interactive and social dynamic of a study group. Oprah certainly did it. That is why we encourage you not to forget the food. Some simple munchies during your meeting warm the tummy and raise the blood sugar after a long day of teaching.

Providing snacks can be done all kinds of ways. Of course, if your study group meets at a restaurant or someone's home, then the food is taken care of. Some-one just needs to call ahead for reservations or the host/ hostess of the home can supply the food (unless every-one brings pot-luck).

If you meet at school, a sign-up sheet can be passed around before the first meeting and participants can volunteer to supply food and drinks. Depending on your facilities, food can be kept warm or cold in the teacher's lounge before the meeting begins. Set-up and clean-up can be the responsibility of those bringing the food for a particular meeting.

If school funds can help offset the price of paper products such as napkins, plates, and utensils, great. If those funds can even pay for the snacks, even better! Someone will need to volunteer to do the shopping. Perhaps there are some PTA moms and dads that will do the cooking for the meetings or some neighborhood restaurants willing to donate a dish or two. It doesn't hurt to ask.

We think the food component of study groups is so appetizing that, as you can see, we have included some favorites in chapter 8. Enjoy!

We hope you find motivating your colleagues to start a study group on campus a delightful challenge rather than an overwhelming task. Remember to be *creative* and *sincere*. Don't overlook those details that can guide your group towards something they are passionate about. You may be pleasantly surprised about what emerges from the study group synergy which is bound to develop.

4

Setting Up Your Study Group

"I looked forward to our book club meetings because of the relaxed setting with plenty of food and snacks. Being able to reflect on what we were reading and to share what was working in our classrooms was a great learning experience. I was inspired to make positive changes in my classroom. My students made real gains as a result."

Rosie Valencia
First grade teacher

You are *Super Educator*!! You eat problems for breakfast, you make 2,500 decisions before lunch, you cure mysterious diseases equipped with nothing but a Band-Aid and some lotion, and you put James Bond's creative thinking skills to shame with the amazing ways you use dried macaroni noodles and brown construction paper.

Unfortunately, even when blessed with what seems like magical powers, you can't do everything. It's the same with setting up your study group. Let's look at the ABCs of your group's set up.

Choosing Materials to Study

Once you have decided on the topic or focus of study, the group or facilitator needs to devise a plan for selecting the study materials. Here are two practical ways of choosing materials.

The facilitator can make the selection and "pitch" the book at a faculty meeting or other staff development meeting. You could put flyers that give a short review of the book in the staff's mailboxes, teachers' lounge, and workroom. Interested teachers could sign up by a designated date. You might even consider sending a personal invitation out to those you know would enjoy reading the book.

Or, the facilitator could provide a number of selections for study. These could be shared with the faculty in the same manner as described above. If you actually have the texts, or can get them from your local library, they can be displayed in the office, teachers' lounge, or any other area the faculty frequent. Put a large sticky note on each book and invite all who are interested to vote by placing a tally or name on the note attached to the book of their choice. The majority wins. If there is a tie between titles, then two study groups can be formed (if possible). Likewise, if a large number (12 or more) of teachers selects the same book, then two meeting dates can be created and the group can be split up. (More on study group size a bit later.)

Setting Up the Ground Rules

Having a set of study group ground rules is as important as having classroom or school rules. Agreed-upon parameters let the participants know the group's expectations for behavior and learning. A study group should be a place where teachers can share their learning and expand their thinking. Tempting as it may be, a study group should not turn into a griping session about the day's frustrations, a conversation about the latest episode of a TV show, or a café where the latest family news is shared. Defined guidelines help keep group members from straying from the topic at hand. Ideally, the study group should be so enthralling it turns into a place where your worries and concerns are willingly left outside the door.

Here are two ways to set up ground rules for your particular group.

The Leader as Catalyst: When Twelve is Too Many to Make a Decision

If you have a set facilitator, that person can be responsible for setting up the ground rules. Keep it simple. Two or three rules are sufficient. No need for the Ten Commandments. The facilitator can set these rules up on his or her own before the first meeting date. They can be given to the participants along with their meeting schedule, readings, and any other necessary information.

The Social Contract: All for One, One for All

A social contract can be drawn up with the group members before the first meeting date. Through discussion, all participants can decide what their expectations are for their learning and discussion time. Together the group will develop their contract or ground rules for the study group.

It might be helpful to create a simple reminder of the rules in written form. Many of us are not fond of being told what to do. Be creative. The rules could be typed on a sheet of paper and placed on the meeting table, written off to one side on the white board in the meeting room, or incorporated into clever bookmarks and given to group members. The rules could be on one side of the bookmark and meeting dates and required readings on the other side.

Whatever method you decide to use, remember the goal is maximum participation by all with a minimum of off-task conversations. Here are some examples of ground rules to choose from:

- Be on time.
- Bring your book and/or journal.
- Complete your reading for the meeting date.
- Be willing to contribute to the discussion.
- Keep cell phones off.
- Share positively.
- Leave the stress of the day at the door.
- No one person should dominate the discussion.
- Allow everyone a chance to share.
- Be respectful of all group members.
- Be reflective of your teaching practices as they relate to the text/materials.
- Keep the focus on the discussion at hand.
- Remember, suffering is optional.

Group Size

How many members should there be? Size does matter. Experts debate ideal study group size; however, they all agree smaller groups tend to work better. IRA's pamphlet *Teachers as Readers Book Groups: Exploring Your Own Literacy* (1997) suggests 10-15 members. However, Carlene Murphy (1999), a contributor to the *Journal of Staff Development* maintains that a study group should consist of no more than six people. We conducted our study group effectively with eleven people, and we think that six to twelve members provide an ideal range.

Our group included teachers from kindergarten, first grade, and second grade. Having teachers from three closely related grade levels allowed us to better understand where our students were coming from and what the expectations for the next grade would be.

In groups larger than twelve it is difficult for members to have equal opportunities to share. Even Oprah kept her book club small. Thousands of viewers may have read the book selection, but only a lucky few met with Oprah and the author for dinner and dialogue. Remember, you want to create a risk-free environment for thoughts and ideas to flow.

If there is tremendous interest in a book, then having several study groups going on at the same time can solve the size problem. This might also help participants who have a conflict with the scheduled meeting dates. Perhaps they could attend another group when a conflict arises. These are all good things to consider when thinking of the size of your study group.

Scheduling: When to Meet

Scheduling can be tricky (another reason to keep the group size small). We recommend initiating a study group at the beginning of a semester or quarter before everyone's schedules are already full. How often the group should meet will depend on the materials being studied and the meetings already blocked into the school calendar. Don't forget to take into account the regularly scheduled staff and committee meetings. Teachers who volunteer for study groups are the same active staff members you see on the social committee, science committee, the campus leadership team, chaperoning the school dance, supervising after school activities, or tutoring.

An easy way to start your study group would be to set up a meeting schedule in advance of the first session. Look at the school calendar and decide how long the group should meet in order to complete the materials. Decide from the table of contents of the book (for multi-media resources check the scope and sequence, teacher's edition, or number/length of videos) what would be a reasonable amount of reading to be done for each meeting. If you schedule a meeting every two weeks, then three chapters might be all you can expect participants to read. If meetings are monthly, longer readings could be completed. If you are studying children's literature, one or two books (depending on the genre) could be completed for *each* meeting.

Remember, you want to keep the interest of the group members going; taking a nine-month period to complete the study of one book could be very frustrating and cause interest to wane. A two-to-three-month period, meeting every other week, is probably sufficient to maintain high interest and complete a professional book or other materials. Larger video series will naturally take longer to complete.

If the book is very dense (i.e. Caulkins, *The Art of Teaching Reading;* Graves, *A Fresh Look at Writing*), you might consider reading only half a book as a study group and allowing the group to finish it on their own. However, if you are like most people, you might need the discipline that scheduled meetings provide to complete longer readings.

Another option for organizing meetings might be to schedule the first meeting in advance, but then decide on the date, time, and readings for subsequent sessions as the group progresses through the study. This requires more flexibility and compromise on the part of the participants and facilitator, but it is certainly do-able (even with our busy schedules and unforeseen appointments).

Where Should You Meet?

A school is certainly the most convenient location for a study group. The library, teacher's lounge, conference room, or classrooms are all practical locations.

Your group might want to meet before school for breakfast at a local restaurant. You could give the group a catchy name like "Books for Breakfast." Restaurants are also a popular choice for after-school meetings. The study group could meet right after school for "happy hour," an early dinner, or evening refreshments. You might even choose to meet on a permanent or rotating basis in people's homes for pot-luck and book talk, swimming and book talk (who's got the pool or hot tub?), or book talk and then a movie.

Finding time to implement a study group *during* the school day might be a bit more difficult and require some creative planning, but it is also a viable option for encouraging school-wide involvement and study. An easy start would be to use designated staff development days to have study groups meet. The problem with this might be the relatively small number of staff development days in the school calendar.

If you meet during the school day, we suggest using paraprofessionals to cover classes for a small group of teachers to meet one hour every two or three weeks. If you can create a rotation schedule using the paraprofessionals, then all classes could be covered in order to allow the entire faculty to participate.

Another option is to create a type of block schedule where students are scheduled for special classes (i.e. music, library, P.E., art, computer lab) at the same time in order to release teachers to meet. Likewise, teachers can coordinate schedules, covering or combining classes for each other for an hour or so to allow study groups to meet during the day.

If weekdays are difficult, weekend meetings are also possible. Meet at the public library, the local park, bookstore, university, or even a spa. It is easy to find a change of scenery. The possibilities are endless.

As you reflect on your own unique study group, remember what the Boy Scouts always say: "Be prepared." It will save time and headaches down the road if all the minor details are planned out in advance.

5

Conducting Your Study Group

*"I enjoyed our book group. Each person in our group
shared valuable information that could be taken back to my
classroom. The book club was a nice way to end a busy day.
There was plenty of laughter, sharing, and tasty treats."*

Rebecca Hough
Second Grade teacher

The books are laid out, the smell of delightfully
sinful munchies fills the air, and the enthusiastic
participants have just arrived. Now what? What
happens during the time your group meets?

Conducting your study group is not rocket science,
but there are a few important factors to consider,
beginning with format. Do you want a structured
session, an informal one, or a balance between the
two? Will the leader/facilitator be permanent, or
rotating? Will follow-up work on the main readings
be expected? How about journaling through the
book study? There are so many possibilities for

conducting a successful study group that we thought we'd take a moment to explore them here.

Who's the Boss?

Every study group needs a leader. Someone has to get the ball rolling (and keep it rolling). This is especially important in the early stages of organization. The leader must be passionate and dedicated to the group. Teachers don't want their study-group time wasted; therefore, to be productive and efficient, it helps to have a leader with a plan.

Most groups choose a permanent facilitator. Oprah is always the facilitator of her book club meetings even though the authors are there to provide their insights. Because Oprah has read the book before the group members are chosen, she can "sell" her audience on giving it a try by her positive testimonial (a real plus). While not always feasible, this strategy is ideal if the facilitator is especially knowledgeable in the material being studied, or reads one or two steps ahead of the rest of the group. For example, if the group topic is some aspect of literacy instruction, your school or district's reading specialist would be the ideal person to lead the group. Likewise, your librarian might be the perfect facilitator if your group is reading current children's literature. Curriculum experts become particularly valuable facilitators when questions arise.

The permanent facilitator takes on the role of setting up the meetings, getting the books, making a schedule, and basically taking care of all the big and small details that go into each meeting. Some ways the leader can facilitate the group are listed below.

Be informed. The facilitator should be aware of area workshops on the topic of study, pertinent websites, or even an online chat with the author of the book. Make it a point to be well informed, as it is your job to keep your group salivating for more.

Plan the agenda ahead of time. It is especially helpful to provide the group members with a schedule or calendar containing dates, times, and readings for all meetings to come. It is also a good way to remind the members about who is bringing the snacks for each meeting.

Be on time and start on time. Simply being there to greet the group as they arrive helps get each session off to a good start. In fact, better to arrive well *ahead* of time to take care of the small details such as setting up the snack table, supplying note-taking materials, and making sure everyone has a place to sit.

Start the discussion and help keep it moving. When time is up, the facilitator sums up the discussion and brings it to a close.

Ask probing questions relevant to the reading. The facilitator needs to be ready with questions to stimulate dialogue during the meetings. We will discuss this in more detail shortly.

Keep the group focused. The facilitator must be tactful and diplomatic to limit digression without discouraging participation. "I know what you mean. So does everyone agree with the statement on page__?" "What you are describing is very similar to what is discussed in today's readings." "Great point, let's get back to...." "I can relate to that. How about..." These are all statements a facilitator might use to refocus the group.

Be the group's cheerleader. A strong facilitator encourages the members to actively make connections with the book and their classrooms. Have teachers share ideas, work samples, or any other thoughts connected to the material being studied and how it works with their students and classrooms.

Bring in related materials. As the facilitator you should be aware of other professional books on the topic of study. If you have access to those books, bring them in to share. Who knows? It might encourage a follow-up book study. Likewise, if charts, blackline masters, or other teaching tools are referenced, and you can provide them for the group, do so.

Reserve time for show-and-tell. This positive strategy always confirms the value of each member and encourages participation by all.

Who's the Boss...This Time?

If, after reading the above job description, you have decided that taking on the role of permanent facilitator is a bit overwhelming, you may choose to have a different leader every time you meet. One person may not be able to lead the group each time. Similarly, the group might prefer to hear a different "voice" conducting each meeting. Or it might simply be easiest to share facilitator duties.

Members must establish the format for this rotating facilitator option before the first meeting. The group can draw numbers, participants can pick the dates they want to lead the group, or facilitators can be nominated by others. One person can agree to get the group off to a successful start, and at the end of the first meeting solicit a volunteer to facilitate for the next one. This can be the closing activity for each subsequent meeting.

Remember that the rotating facilitator's job description is the same as the permanent facilitator's. He or she must take care of all the big and small details of conducting a successful group. Think about the personalities of your group members before you commit to a shared leadership role. If there is not an "all for one and one for all" type of commitment, this might not work.

Question Stems to Promote Discussion

If you are worried about having meaningful book conversations or creating structure for your discussions, having a set of questions to reflect upon is a good way to start. Richard Allington's *What Really Matters for Struggling Readers* provides some general question stems that would work for just about any type of study group. Your question stems can be written ahead of time on the board in the meeting room so that no time will be wasted when the group convenes. They could also be run off and included with a friendly reminder about the upcoming meeting. This could be given to the teachers a couple of days before the next meeting. All the group members would have their own copy and could refer to them if needed. Some examples of general broad-based questions are

- What was the author suggesting?

- How is this information relevant in the classroom and pertinent to my teaching?

- What do you still have questions about and what would you like to learn more about?

- What strategies, concepts, or ideas from the text have you applied in your classroom?

- What did you learn from using these ideas or strategies in your classroom? What would you improve upon or do differently next time?

If your group wants questions that address your particular topic of study, the facilitator must plan ahead and develop a few questions that connect the readings to your group's membership, classrooms, and schools. Keep in mind that many professional books on the market today already include questions and suggestions for professional development at the end of each chapter.

Remember, less is more. No need for multi-page standardized test forms and number two pencils. A few meaningful questions suffice to get things going. Your group might surprise you though; sometimes members find enough to talk about without ever looking at the questions you supplied.

First and Last Responder

Another option to get your discussion going is to have a "first responder." It is the first responder's job to open up the study by asking the first question, sharing the first comment or opinion, or reading the first journal entry (see below, "Journaling"). This helps eliminate awkwardness, hesitation, or reluctance to share.

Similarly, the "last responder's" job is to wrap things up and keep track of time. When the session is coming to an end, the last responder shares a few summary statements, last comments, or parting questions. That is the signal that the study group time together is concluded. The last responder can also remind everyone when and where the next meeting is, who is bringing snacks, chapters to be read, etc. The group can choose the next meeting's first and last responders by drawing names from a hat. This can be done either after the last bit of business, or at the onset of the meeting. In this way everyone knows his or her role, and the meeting can flow smoothly.

Journaling

Journaling is a useful way to encourage self-reflection as teachers voyage through a book study. It is an effective way for each member to focus on professional growth and understanding separate from the formal meetings.

Before the group begins, give each participant the book to be studied and a journal. If your group can find the funds, provide bound journals (rather than spiral notebooks) from your local bookstore. If you go the spiral notebook route, get creative and decorate them with a catchy name for your group, or use another clever way to personalize.

As the members go through the readings for each session, encourage each to share their thoughts in their journals. To start things off at each meeting, the facilitator can invite a few to share their jottings. This will get the discussion started without having to supply question prompts.

The IRA Literacy Study Groups Facilitator's Guide provides some questions teachers may use when making personal observations about the study group or any other activities related to it. You may obtain a copy by going to their web site at www.reading.org.

A modified way to do some journaling is to have the facilitator create a handout with questions and reflections specific for each of the readings. (See "Who's The Boss" earlier in this chapter, for examples.) You might even want to leave room for notes on your handout so teachers can record any classroom successes they have experienced specific to their readings.

Let's Practice What We Read

We teachers already have more than enough to keep us busy, without extra reading. Yet our study group experience showed how even a "skinny" book can yield wonderful, and fairly immediate, results. Many professional books now on the market share teaching strategies, lesson plans, and other extremely useful activities. Some even have videotapes that demonstrate the lessons in the companion book.

As a part of the book study, participants can be required to try an activity, lesson, or strategy with their class (see chapter 1, Practices Study Group). At the next meeting the members can report on how it went. It's like having show-and-tell at the onset of each meeting. Teachers can bring writing samples, lesson materials, teaching aids, or anything else they would like to share.

One type of follow-up assignment would be to have a teacher volunteer to videotape the lesson he/she tried out. What a fabulous learning tool for the rest of the group! This show-and-tell time allows teachers to brag about their successes and also to get help troubleshooting when they encounter glitches. Actually seeing what other teachers are attempting might encourage members in the group to try some new ideas.

Time's up!

How long is long enough for a study group meeting? It will depend on a number of factors:

- How much reading is done for each meeting?

- Are you having a meal with the study or just snacks?

- The more participants, the more time must be provided for everyone to have an opportunity to share.

- Are you showing videotapes along with the book discussion?

- Are you sharing journal reflections?

- Did you bring materials for show-and-tell?

With our busy schedules, an hour meeting might be all the time your group can spare. On the other hand, an hour might not be enough to cover the readings. Most study groups meet from one to two hours. If it goes longer you are probably enjoying a great meal and fellowship along with the book talk.

Whatever length you decide on, stick to it. If necessary, appoint someone to be the timekeeper. That person can give the facilitator the "two minute warning" to wrap things up and draw the meeting to a close. It is our hope that your book study will be so successful that you will find yourselves saying, "Where did the time go? It seems like we barely started."

Remember: every group is unique. You must decide (sometimes through trial and error) what works best for you. Take these ideas and devise a plan for your particular needs. A framework to work from contributes to a successful study group.

6

After the Study Group…What Next?

"It was so encouraging to find that some of the things I felt were failed attempts in my classroom were really great beginnings. Talking, reflecting, and reading made me see where I could improve, and how to go forward."

Frankie Wiseman
Second Grade teacher

You have just finished your last session of a three-month study group. Your highlighted, note-filled, dog-eared book has been closed. As you reflect upon all your meetings, you might be saying to yourself, "That was great, but what now? Am I ever going to use this in my classroom?"

The answer is a resounding *yes*! The more you put into a study group, the more you get out of it. So, before you put that professional journal back on the shelf never to open it again, let's explore the ways we can take what we have learned during our time together and "run with it."

What kinds of additional activities can we apply to our study? How can we encourage and promote a transfer of new teaching ideas to the classroom as well as "infect" the rest of the faculty with the enthusiasm and motivation for professional growth that study groups provide?

Revisit the Book

The best place to start is at the beginning. Go back to your first study group session and skim over your notes and the material you read. Highlight the most important concepts you learned, and choose one (yes, only one!) strategy you would like to work on. Get all the materials and lesson components ready before you begin experimenting with it in the classroom. When everything is in place, give it a try. If you like, have a fellow group member observe you teach and/or videotape the lesson. When done you might want to make some anecdotal notes in your journal as to the success or failure of the lesson, or debrief with a study group colleague.

When you are comfortable with the way you have implemented the teaching technique you chose, build on it. Continue reviewing your journal. Go to your notes for the second study group session and find another idea or strategy which complements the one you just put into place. Repeat the above process until you have implemented everything you can from the book.

Keep in mind that sustaining this level of self-reflection requires stamina. To systematically incorporate study group findings into your teaching routine requires discipline on your part, and you may struggle to stay on task if you embark on the project alone. Consider collaborating with another study group member. The two of you can hold each other accountable to your goals by sharing ideas, reflecting on the lessons taught, and encouraging one another to try new ideas from the study.

Develop a Curriculum

As you and your colleagues slowly incorporate the ideas you learned from your study group into your teaching, you could also create a working "teacher's edition" on the topic you studied. When we had our book study on Marcia Freeman's *Teaching the Youngest Writer*s, we correlated her strategies with our school district's scope and sequence for writing. We created binders that became our teacher's guide for writing for the school year. Our student expectations as per state mandates were aligned with the strategies found in the book and were organized for each nine-week grading period. We also included teaching aids, materials, and any other resources to help complete the lessons.

Your teacher's guide could include the following:
• **Lesson Ideas.** You can take lesson ideas directly from the book, or customize lessons from the book study to fit your particular grade level or subject taught. You could organize the lessons as we did, in binders with dividers for each reporting period or subject, or any other way that works for you. The idea is to have a practical, hands-on tool that you can grab and use.

• **Objectives.** It is very important to align the contents of your teacher's guide with your school district's objectives and student expectations. Take the time at the onset to do this and it will facilitate lesson planning throughout the year.

• **Materials.** Add to your guide any materials you may need to teach the lessons. This could include visual aids, transparencies, or student work samples to use as models. You can even include assessment tools and rubrics.

• **References.** Here is where you can insert related literature and multimedia resources to help teach the lessons. Pertinent websites or other professional books on the subject can also be useful information.

Not only is a teacher's guide a practical way to make connections with the text, but it also extends the mean-ingful dialogue generated around the book. Some study groups add sessions after the book has been completed precisely because they want to develop a curriculum specific to their school's needs. If the whole group pitches in to help in the design and development of the guide, the task will go much more smoothly. "Two heads are better than one" definitely applies in this case. When completed and enclosed in a binder, your teacher's guide becomes a handy reference that can easily be modified and extended as the need arises.

One Good Study Group Leads to Another

After completing one successful book study, you might crave more. An easy way to build on your rapidly expanding expertise is to begin investigating another book on the same topic. Perhaps you have just finished a fabulous three-month study on literature circles. Find another book on the topic and continue. Better yet, find a videotape on literature circles such as Harvey Daniels, *Literature Circles: Voice and Choice in Book Clubs and Literature Circles* and expand your study with that. Viewing the actual practice of literature circles would be a superb complement to the just-completed reading of a book on the topic. Take it one step further and each member can videotape him- or herself conducting a literature circle session in the classroom. Bring it back to the next study group session for a review by the members. If you or a member of the group is extremely resourceful, locate the author's e-mail address or phone number (start with the publishing company), set up an on-line chat or conference call, and have a little question-and-answer session.

You might enjoy reading a professional book by a particular author so much that you choose to read another book by that same author. Look into other titles he/she has written. If you can, find copies of the books to examine with the group before choosing one. If not, get recommendations from someone who has read the titles, or look for reviews in professional journals and/or amazon.com.

This would also be the perfect opportunity to get others to join the next installment of your book club. Capitalize on the ever-growing excitement of the study group and "pitch" the new selection at a faculty meeting or other appropriate occasion as suggested in chapter 4, "Choosing Materials to Study." Your next study group is bound to acquire some new members. Better yet, there might be such enthusiasm to embrace this new means of professional development that there will be several groups going on simultaneously at your school.

Develop a TIP Group

Devouring everything you can on the topic of study can lead to a TIP group. Teacher Inquiry Projects (TIP) could be conducted in teams of two teachers or more depending on the area of teacher research to be conducted. Mary Ann Van Tassell says "Getting involved in teacher research is a form of professional development that enables teachers to be a part of a reflective discourse that extends beyond the classroom" (as cited in Irwin, 2002 p. 20).

Teacher inquiry research can be done on

- The topic of your study group and what research says about it.

- Individual teaching practices as they relate to the topic of study.

- Grade-level or school-wide teaching practices and their relation to the topic of study and/or student achievement.

- Connections between the topic of study and existing school programs, policy, and curriculum.

- Individual student learning and its relation to teaching practices.

The area of study you are interested in will guide the manner in which your research is carried out. There is not one fixed method for this. As mentioned in chapter 1, Allington's *What Really Matters for Struggling Readers* and *IRA's Facilitators Guide* both provide a number of resources to help you get started on teacher inquiry and research. Lyons and Pinnell's *Systems for Change in Literacy Education* also offer some simple steps in getting started. However you choose to extend your study group through research, the excitement comes in the changes and improvements made both individually and school-wide.

Hear Ye, Hear Ye

A terrific follow-up to your study group would be to let everyone know what they missed. Put out a study group newsletter. Give it a catchy name, print it on colorful paper, and circulate it to the faculty and staff. The contents of the newsletter, of course, will depend on the unique nature of your study. It could include pertinent information from the book, teacher conversations, or information gained from the videotapes. Offer some lesson ideas or strategies that everyone can use. Add quotes and testimonials from the members, a study group recipe or two, and you're sure to whet the appetite of non-members to join the next time around.

Ongoing newsletters also work well. This requires extra commitment on the part of the facilitator (or perhaps a volunteer group member or two), but it is an exciting way to spread the news. After every group session, write the newsletter. In this way you are keeping a continuing dialogue with the faculty that extends beyond the study group meetings.

A bulletin board serves the same purpose as a newsletter and is less time-consuming to produce. Change out the information displayed on it after every meeting, and *voila*! It achieves everything the newsletter does. The bulletin board will also communicate—to students, parents, and visitors to the school—your positive ethos: Improved teacher expertise creates improved student success. Learning never ends.

If your school has a web page, consider adding information about your study group there. Likewise, submit information about the success of your study group to your school district's web page and/or newsletter. This will lead you to our next suggestion.

Share the Wealth

In the midst of all the reflecting your group has been doing, why not write an article about your study group experience? Get published. There are numerous educational journals as well as Web sites that encourage and accept teacher submissions. Some publications to consider are *Reading Teacher, Instructor, Elementary School Journal,* and *Language Arts* (to name a very few). Check out your local and state reading associations or educational agencies. Visit their Web sites, see what they publish, and consider submitting an article for publication.

Write a proposal to present the "nuts and bolts" of starting a successful study group at an educational conference. Presenting at a conference is an effective way to share how easy it is to get a study group started. Bring along a few group members to put a "face" to your group as well as provide some personal reflections.

You might also consider developing a workshop around the knowledge learned from your study group. Presenting an in-service about the effective strategies you learned and their classroom applications will solidify your expertise and strengthen the knowledge base of other teachers. Make sure you emphasize to other faculty how the learning grew out of focused conversations around the book. Think of your presentation as a way to promote and encourage wider membership in the next study group to be formed.

Cloning Your Group

Speaking of wider membership, why not start study groups at other schools? Here are some ways to get the word out.

- Present your idea to the administration at a nearby school. If the administration likes the idea, share it at a faculty meeting. If the study group is a "go," and a facilitator is appointed, help in whatever way necessary to get the group off to a successful start.

- Consider presenting at regularly scheduled school or district administrative meetings to generate interest in district-wide study groups.

- Create a videotape that you can send around to be viewed at other schools.

- Try mentoring a novice study group.

- Collaborate and partner with another school in setting up a wider membership in a new study. This provides networking opportunities and allows two schools to share the responsibilities of maintaining the group.

- Try a district-wide, on-line study group.

- If other schools are studying the same book as your group, set up a "share night" where everyone can come together for book talk and an exchange of ideas.

- Put out a district newsletter where all the locations, times, and topics of study are listed throughout your district. Allow teachers and administrators membership in whatever group meets their needs.

Remember to keep the communication going long after your group has ended. It is through that communication that knowledge builds. As J.M. Irwin says, "Sharing is a potential for starting new conversations, developing new theories, asking new questions, creating new possibilities, and forming new communities of learners" (Irwin, 2002). There are a myriad of ways to continue communicating and developing professionally as a result of a study group. It really comes down to choosing a way that meets your interest, time, available resources, and motivational needs. Enjoy the journey!

7

Quick Reference Checklist

I'm making a list and checking it twice...

Getting Started

- Choose a topic based on some type of needs assessment

- Research relevant titles

- Purchase the books and/or journals

- Choose a group leader

- Get permission on possible teacher professional development credits and/or incentives

Before First Meeting

- Reserve a room on campus/ at restaurant

- Prepare a sign-in sheet

- Develop a set of ground rules

- Put a reminder in the teacher's mailboxes a few days before the meeting

- Make a schedule of the meeting dates

- Divide up the chapters to be read for each meeting date

- Have audio/visual equipment ready if needed

- Have enough chairs/tables/work area for the group

- Prepare focus questions

What the Facilitator Brings to the Meeting

- Study group rules

- Markers

- Sticky notes

- Stapler

- Pens/pencils

- Sample lessons

- Work samples

- Focus questions

What the Participants Bring to the Meeting

- Book and/or journal with readings completed

- Work samples (if applicable)

- Questions/comments

- Snacks (if it is your turn)

Refreshment Corner

Don't forget the essentials

- Plates

- Bowls

- Cups

- Napkins

- Utensils

- Drinks

- Trash can/bags

- Ice Chest

Book Suggestions for specific study topics
READING

- *The Art of Teaching Reading,* by Lucy Calkins. Pearson Education, 2000.

- *Guided Reading: Good First Teaching for All Children,* by Gay Su Pinnell and Irene Fountas. Heinemann, 1996.

- *Guided Read & Writers (3-6),* by Gay Su Pinnell and Irene Fountas. Heinemann, 2000.

- *In the Middle: New Understanding About Writing, Reading, and Learning*, by Nancie Atwell. Heinemann, 1998.

- *Mosaic of Thought: Teaching Comprehension in a Reader's Workshop*, by Susan Zimmermann and Ellen Oliver Keene. Heinemann, 1997.

- *On Solid Ground: Strategies for Teaching Reading K-3*, by Sharon Taberski. Heinemann, 2000.

- *Reading Reminders: Tools, Tips, and Techniques*, by Jim Burke and Lois Bridges Bird. Heinemann, 2000.

- *Reading With Meaning: Teaching Comprehension in the Primary Grades*, by Debbie Miller. Stenhouse, 2002.

- *Scaffolding Reading Experiences*, by Michael Graves and Bonnie Graves. Christopher-Gordon Publishing, 2003.

- *Strategies That Work: Teaching Comprehension to Enhance Understanding*, by Stephanie Harvey and Anne Goudvis. Stenhouse, 2000.

- *Supporting Struggling Readers and Writers: Strategies for Classroom Intervention 3-6,* by Dorothy S. Strickland, Kathy Ganske, and Joanne K. Monroe. Stenhouse, 2001.

- *Teaching Struggling Readers*, by Richard Allington. International Reading Association, 2000.

WRITING

- *A Fresh Look at Writing*, by Donald H. Graves. Heinemann, 1994.

- *Acts of Teaching: How to Teach Writing: A Text, A Reader, A Narrative,* by Joyce Armstrong Carroll and Edward E. Wilson. Libraries Unlimited, 1993.

- *Building a Writing Community*, by Marcia S. Freeman. Maupin House Publishing, 1995.

- *Craft Lessons: Teaching Writing K through 8*, by Ralph J. Fletcher and JoAnn Portalupi. Stenhouse Publishers, Sept. 1998.

- *Interactive Writing: How Language; Literacy Come Together, K-2,* by Andrea McCarrier, Gay Su Pinnell, and Irene C. Fountas. Heinimann, 1999.

- *Never Too Early to Write: Adventures in the K-1 Writing Workshop, by* Bea Johnson. Maupin House Publishing, 1999.

- *Nonfiction Craft Lessons: Teaching Writing K-8*, by JoAnn Portalupi and Ralph J. Fletcher. Stenhouse, 2001.

- *Nonfiction Writing Strategies: Using Science Big Books as Models,* by Marcia S. Freeman. Maupin House Publishing, 2000.

- *Scaffolding Young Writers: A Writer's Workshop Approach*, by Linda J. Dorn and Carla Loffos. Stenhouse Publishers, 2001.

- *Teaching the Youngest Writers: A Practical Guide*, by Marcia S. Freeman. Maupin House Publishing, 1999.

- *The Art of Teaching Writing*, by Lucy McCormick Calkins and Peter Cunningham. Heinemann, 1995.

- *What a Writer Needs*, by Ralph J. Fletcher, Forward by Donald M. Murray. Elsevier, Reed, Incorporated, 1992.

- *Writing Workshop: The Essential Guide from the Authors of Craft Lessons*, by Ralph J. Fletcher and JoAnn Portalupi. Heinemann, 2001.

LITERACY CENTERS

- *Literacy Work Stations: Making Centers Work*, by Debbie Diller. Stenhouse Publishers, 2003.

- *Primary Literacy Centers: Making Reading and Writing Stick!* By Susan Nations and Mellissa Alonso. Maupin House Publishing, 2001.

- *The Literacy Center: Contexts for Reading and Writing,* by Lesley Mandel Morrow. Stenhouse Publishers, 1997.

- *The Teacher's Guide to Four Blocks: A Multimethod, Multilevel Framework for Grades 1-3,* by Patricia M. Cunningham, Dorothy P. Hall, and Cheryl M. Sigmon. Carson-Dellosa, 1999.

- *What Are the Other Kids Doing While You Teach Small Groups?* By Donna Marriott, Joel Kupperstein, Carolea Williams, and Gwen Connelly. Creative Teaching Press, 1997.

PHONEMIC AWARENESS, PHONICS & SPELLING

- *For the Love of Language: Poetry for Every Learner*, by Nancy Lee Cecil. Peguis Publishers, 1994.

- *Phonemic Awareness in Young Children: A Classroom Curriculum*, by Marilyn Jager Adams, Ingvor Lindberg, Barbara R. Foorman, and Terri Beeler. Paul H. Brookes, Publisher, 1998.

- *Phonics They Use: Words for Reading and Writing*, by Patricia Marr Cunningham. Addison-Wesley, 1999.

- *Systematic Sequential Phonics They Use: For Beginning Readers of All Ages*, by Patricia M. Cunningham. Carson-Dellosa, 2000.

- *Voices on Word Matters: Learning about Phonics and Spelling in the Literacy Classroom*, by Irene C. Fountas and Gay Su Pinnell. Heinemann, 1999.

- *Word Journeys*, by Kathy Ganske. Guilford Publications, Inc., 2000.

- *Word Matters: Teaching Phonics and Spelling in the Reading/Writing Classroom*, by Gay Su Pinnell, Irene C. Fountas, and Mary E. Giacobbe. Heinemann, 1998.

- *Words, Words, Words: Teaching Vocabulary in Grades 4-12*, by Janet Allen. Stenhouse, 1999.

- *Words Their Way: Word Study for Phonics, Vocabulary, and Spelling Instruction*, by Donald R. Bear, Francine Johnston, Shane Tampleta, and Marcia Invernizzi. Prentice Hall Professional Technical Reference, 2003.

DIFFERENTIATED INSTRUCTION

- *By Different Paths to Common Outcomes*, by Marie M. Clay. Stenhouse Publishers, 1998.

- *Different Brains, Different Learners: How to Reach the Hard to Reach,* by Eric Jensen. The Brain Store, Incorporated, 2000.

- *Differentiated Instruction: Different Strategies for Different Learners*, by Char Forsten, Jim Grant, and Betty Hollas. Staff Development for Educators, 2002.

- *Differentiated Instruction in the Regular Class-room: How to Reach and Teach All Learners, Grades 3-12*, by Diane Heacox. Free Spirit Publishing, Inc., 2001.

- *Teaching With the Brain in Mind*, by Eric Jensen. Association for Supervision and Curriculum Development, 1998.

SCHOOL WIDE CHANGE

- *Balanced Literacy Instruction: A Teachers' Resource Book*, by Kathryn H. Au, Judith A. Scherr, and Jacqueline H. Carroll. Christopher-Gordon Publishers, 2001.

- *Classrooms That Work: They Can All Read and Write*, by Patricia Marr Cunningham and Richard L. Allington. Pearson Education, 2002.

- *First Days of School: How to be an Effective Teacher*, by Harry K. Wong. Harry K.Wong 2001.

- *Mentoring Beginning Teachers: Guiding, Reflecting, Coaching*, by Jean Boreen, Donna Niday, Mary K. Johnson, and Joe Potts. Stenhouse, 2000.

- *Redefining Staff Development: A Collaborative Model for Teachers and Administration*, by Laura Robb. Heinemann, 2000.

- *Schools That Work: Where All Children Read and Write, Vol. 2,* by Richard L. Allington and Patricia M. Cunningham. Pearson Education, 2001.

- *Systems for Change in Literacy Education: A Guide to Professional Development*, by Carol A. Lyons and Gay Su Pinnell. Heinemann, 2001.

- *Testing is Not Teaching: What Should Count in Education*, by Donald H. Graves. Heinemann, 2002.

LANGUAGE

- *A Project Approach to Language Learning: Linking Literary Genres and Themes in Elementary Classrooms*, by Katherine Luongo-Orlando. Stenhouse, 2001.

- *Scaffolding Language, Scaffolding Learning: Teaching Second Language Learners in the Mainstream Classroom*, by Pauline Gibbons. Heinemann, 2002.

- *Second Language Learners*, by Marie M. Clay. Stenhouse, 1997

LEADERSHIP

- *FISH! A Remarkable Way to Boost Morale and Improve Results,* Stephen C. Lundin, John Christensen, Harry Paul, Hyperion Press, 2000.

- *If You Don't Feed the Teachers They Eat the Students: Guide to Success for Administrators and Teachers*, by Neila A. Connors. Incentive Publications, 2000.

- *Nothing's Impossible: Leadership Lessons from Inside and Outside the Classroom*, by Lorraine Monroe. Public Affairs, 1999.

- *Results: The Key to Continuous School Improvement*, by Michael J. Schmoker. Association for Supervision and Curriculum Development, 1999.

- *The Courage to Teach: A Guide for Reflection and Renewal*, by Rachel C. Livsey and Parker J. Palmer. Jossey-Bass, 1999.

- *The Literacy Principal: Leading, Supporting, and Assessing Reading and Writing Initiatives*, by David Booth, Michael Fullan, and Jennifer Rowell. Stenhouse, 2002.

MATH

- *About Teaching Mathematics: A K-8 Resource*, by Marilyn Burns. Math Solutions Publications, 1998.

- *Elementary & Middle School Mathematics: Teaching Developmentally*, by John A. VanDeWalle. Pearson Education, 2003.

- *Everyday Math for the Numerically Challenged*, by Audrey Carlan. Career Press, 1998.

- *Math: Facing an American Phobia*, by Marilyn Burns. Math Solutions Publications, Feb. 1998.

- *Math & Literature: K-3 Vol. 1*, by Marilyn Burns. Math Solutions Publications, Jan. 1993.

- *Math as a Way of Knowing*, by Susan Ohanian. Stenhouse, 1996.

SCIENCE/SOCIAL STUDIES

- *Botany of Desire: A Plant's-Eye View of the World*, by Michael Pollan. The Random House Publishing Group, 2001.

- *Drop of Water: A Book of Science and Wonder*, by Walter Wick. Scholastic, Inc., 1997.

- *If This is Social Studies, Why Isn't it Boring?* By Stephanie Steffey and Wendy J. Hood (Editor). Stenhouse, 1994.

- *Learning Together Through Inquiry: From Columbus to Integrated Curriculum*, by Kathy

Gnagey Short, Jean Schroeder, Julie Laird, Gloria Kauffman, and Margaret J. Ferguson. Stenhouse, 1996.

- *Literature and Science Breakthroughs: Connecting Language and Science Skills in the Elementary Classroom*, by Jo-Anne Lake. Stenhouse, 2000.

- *Science Times Book of the Brain: The Best Science Reporting from the Acclaimed Weekly Section of the New York Times*, by Nicholas Wade (Editor). The Lyons Press, 1998.

- *Taking Inquiry Outdoors: Reading, Writing, and Science Beyond the Classroom Walls*, by Barbara Bourne. Stenhouse, 1999.

- *Teaching Reading in Social Studies, Science, and Math*, by Laura Robb and Judy Lynch. Scholastic, Inc., 2002.

- *The Science of Harry Potter: How Magic Really Works*, by Roger Highfield. Penguin USA, 2003.

VIDEO TAPE SERIES
- *Close-up Look at Teaching Reading* (4 tapes), by Sharon Taberski. Heinemann, 1995.

- *Happy Reading* (3 tapes), by Debbie Miller. Stenhouse Publishers, 2002.

- *Inside Reading & Writing Workshops* (4 tapes), by Joanne Hindley. Stenhouse, 1998.

- *Looking into Literature Circles*, by Harvey Daniels. Stenhouse, 2001.

- *Marcia Freeman's K-5 School-wide Writing Program* (16 tapes), by Marcia S. Freeman. Maupin House Publishing, 2003.

- *Organizing for Literacy* (4 tapes), by Linda J. Dorn. Stenhouse, 1999.

- *Primary Literacy Video Collection*, by Irene C. Fountas and Gay Su Pinnell. Heinemann.

  Guided Reading – 2 tapes, July, 2001.

  Classroom Management – 2 tapes, 2001.

  Word Study – 2 tapes, 2002.

- *Results That Last* (4 tapes), by Linda J. Dorn and Carla Soffos. Stenhouse Publishers, 2003.

- *Snapshots,* by Linda Hoyt. Heinemann, 2000.

- *Strategy Instruction in Action*, by Stephanie Harvey and Anne Goudvis. Stenhouse Publishers, 2001.

- *When Students Write*, by Ralph J. Fletcher and JoAnn Portalupi. Stenhouse, 2002.

- *Focus on Spelling,* Snowball (4 tapes), by Diane Snowball. Stenhouse, 2000.

HOME/SCHOOL CONNECTION

- *Families at Work: A Guide for Educators, Vol.1*, by Adele Thomas, Lynn Fazio, and Betty L. Stiefelmeyer. International Reading Association, 1999.

- *Family Literacy: From Theory to Practice*, by Andrea Debruin-Parecki, and Barbara Krol-Sinclair (Editors). International Reading Association, 2003.

- *More than Bake Sales: The Resource Guide to Family Involvement in Education*, by James Vopat, Pete Leki. Stenhouse, 1998.

- *Read it Aloud: A Parent's Guide to Sharing Books with Young Children*, by Monty Haas and Laurie Joy Haas. The Reading Railroad, 2000.

- *Teachers and Parents Together*, by Maureen Botrie. Pembroke, 1992.

8

Great Study Group Munchies

Cool Veggie Pizza

8-ounce package crescent rolls

8 ounces cream cheese, softened
1 ½ teaspoons mayonnaise
1 clove garlic, finely minced
1 teaspoon dill mix
salt and pepper to taste

2 cups assorted fresh veggies: carrots, cucumbers, broccoli, green/red bell peppers, tomatoes, onions, mushrooms, etc.

1 ounce (¼ cup) cheddar cheese, shredded

Spread crescent rolls on pizza pan and bake.
Combine cream cheese, mayo, dill, salt, and
pepper and spread over the cooled, galic
crescent rolls. Place veggies on top, sprinkle
the cheese, cut and serve.

Hot Cheese Dip

2 pounds Velveeta® Cheese
2 cans chili (no beans)
1 can Hot RO*TEL® Diced Tomatoes and Green
Chillies

Put all in large crock pot and heat. Serve over chips.

Snowballs

1 tub nondairy whipped topping
1 tub sour cream
bananas

1 package flaked coconut

Combine both whipped topping and sour cream.
Slice bananas in 1-inch sections and dip each into the
above mixture. Roll in coconut and serve.

Tortilla Wraps #1

8 ounces cream cheese
4 teaspoons ranch salad dressing mix – dry
1 package dried shredded beef
½ cup broccoli, finely chopped
½ cup cauliflower, finely chopped
¼ cup green onion, finely chopped
¼ cup black olives, finely chopped
5 flour tortillas

Combine all ingredients and spread over tortillas.
Wrap each tortilla into a roll and refrigerate. Cut in
bite-sized pieces and serve.

Watergate Salad

1 large tub of nondairy whipped topping
1 package pistachio pudding

1 can crushed pineapple
2 cups miniature marshmallows

chopped pecans (optional)

Mix whipped topping and pudding together. Add pineapple, marshmallows and nuts. Ready to serve.

Cucumber Salad

1 small package lime gelatin

1 cucumber, grated
1 small onion, finely chopped
1 cup cottage cheese
½ cup nuts
½ cup mayonnaise

Prepare gelatin according to package directions. When gelatin has set, stir in remaining ingredients and mix well.

Dang Good Pie

6 eggs
3 cups sugar
1 ¾ sticks margarine

1 cup crushed pineapple, drained

1 cup flaked coconut
1 cup chopped pecans

1 teaspoon vanilla

Preheat oven to 350°. Beat margarine, sugar and eggs together. Add pineapple, coconut and pecans. Mix well. Add vanilla. Pour into 9" pie crust (unbaked). Bake for 45 minutes.

Bacon Crackers

Preheat oven to 275°. Wrap ½ slice bacon around narrow side of club cracker and fasten with a toothpick. Place on broiler pan and bake for 25 minutes.

Chip Dip

8 ounces cream cheese

¼ cup salad olives
1 teaspoon onion, grated

1 tablespoon lemon juice
milk

corn or other favorite chip

Beat cream cheese until smooth. Finely chop salad olives and grate onion. Add to cream cheese. Add lemon juice and just enough milk to make dip a smooth consistency. Serve with chips.

Pineapple Punch

1 quart pineapple juice
12 ounces Fresca®

Mix and serve at once. This keeps well in the refrigerator.

Fresh Fruit Medley with Poppy Seed Dressing

1 fresh pineapple

1 cup fresh banana slices
1 cup chopped unpeeled apple
1 cup chopped, seeded orange
1 cup chopped cantaloupe
sugar to taste
poppy seed dressing

Cut pineapple in half lengthwise. Scoop out pineapple pulp to form shells. Cut pulp into chunks. Combine with remaining fruits and sugar in bowl; mix well. Spoon into pineapple shells. Serve with Poppy Seed Dressing.

Poppy Seed Dressing

½ cup sugar
1 teaspoon dry mustard
1 teaspoon salt
¼ teaspoon grated onion

1/3 cup vinegar

1 cup oil
1 tablespoon poppy seeds

Combine first 4 ingredients in bowl. Add a small amount of vinegar to moisten; mix well. Add oil and remaining vinegar gradually, beating until thick. Mix in poppy seeds.

Party Chicken Salad Balls

1 cup chopped, cooked chicken
1 tablespoon chopped green onion
2 tablespoons chopped pimento
dash of bottled hot sauce
½ cup salad dressing
1 cup chopped pecans

Combine all ingredients in bowl; mix well. Chill for several hours. Shape into 1-inch balls; arrange on serving plate. Yields 2 dozen.

Cheese Ball

4 cups (1 pound) shredded cheddar cheese
4 (3-ounce) packages cream cheese
½ cup chopped, pimento-stuffed olives
3 tablespoons mayonnaise
$1/_8$ teaspoon celery salt
½ teaspoon Worcestershire sauce
2 tablespoons minced onions
dash of garlic salt

chopped parsley
sliced, pimento-stuffed olives
chopped pecans

Combine first 8 ingredients. Garnish with remaining ingredients.

Molded Strawberry Gelatin

2 small packages strawberry gelatin
1 cup boiling water
2 packages (12-ounces each) frozen strawberries, thawed
1 can (16 oz) crushed pineapple, drained
3 medium bananas, mashed
1 cup chopped walnuts
1 cup sour cream or cream cheese (optional)

Dissolve gelatin in boiling water. Fold in strawberries and juice, drained pineapple, bananas and walnuts. Turn ½ into mold. Refrigerate until firm. Spread top with sour cream. Spoon on rest of strawberry mixture and refrigerate.

Tortilla Wraps #2

1 package large tortillas
8 ounces cream cheese
1 ½ packages taco seasoning
8 ounces sour cream
1 cup cheddar cheese
1 bunch green onions, chopped
3 tablespoons salsa
dash garlic powder

Blend first four ingredients. Add remaining ingredients and mix.
Spread on tortillas and roll up. Chill for at least 2 hours before you cut them up.

Chex® Party Mix Recipe

6 tablespoons butter or margarine
4 teaspoons Worcestershire sauce
1 teaspoon seasoned salt

2 cups Wheat Chex® cereal
2 cups Rice Chex® cereal
2 cups Corn Chex® cereal
¾ cups salted nuts

Preheat oven to 250°. Melt butter in a large shallow pan over low heat. Stir in Worcestershire and seasoned salt. Add the cereals and nuts. Mix over low heat until all pieces are coated. Heat for 45 minutes in the oven, stirring every 15 minutes. Spread out on absorbent paper to cool. Yields 6 ¾ cups.

Spinach and Artichoke Dip

9 ounces frozen creamed spinach, thawed
¾ cup freshly grated Parmesan cheese (reserve ¼ cup for topping)
14-ounce can artichoke hearts, drained and chopped
¼ teaspoon white pepper
1 teaspoon fresh lemon juice
1 cup mozzarella cheese, shredded

Preheat oven to 350°. Combine all the ingredients and blend thoroughly. Place in an ovenproof dish. Top with remaining Parmesan cheese. Cover and refrigerate. Bake dip until hot and bubbly. Serve with your favorite chips.

Zucchini Spread

1 cup grated sharp cheddar cheese
1 cup grated zucchini
¾ cup mayonnaise
½ cup chopped walnuts
1 teaspoon fresh lemon juice

assorted crackers or crudités

Combine cheese, zucchini, mayonnaise, walnuts and lemon juice in medium bowl. Refrigerate 1 hour or overnight. Transfer to serving dish. Serve with assorted crackers or crudités.

Mango Gelatin Mold

1 package lemon gelatin
1 can mango nectar or juice
6 ounces cream cheese
1 cup boiling water

Combine all ingredients in blender and cool in refrigerator. Pour into mold.

Sugar and Honey Pecans

1 ½ cup sugar
½ cup water
¼ cup honey
¼ teaspoon salt

½ teaspoon vanilla extract

3 cups pecan halves

Combine first 4 ingredients in a saucepan; mix well. Cook mixture over medium heat, stirring constantly, until sugar dissolves. Continue cooking, without stirring, until mixture reaches soft ball stage (240 °). Remove from heat; stir in vanilla. Beat with a wooden spoon until mixture begins to thicken. Stir in pecans. Pour mixture onto waxed paper and separate pecans. Cool. Yields 4 cups.

References

Allington, R.L. (2001). *What really matters for struggling readers: designing research-based programs*. Boston, MA: Addison-Wesley Educational Publishers, Inc.

Calkins, L.M. (2001). *The art of teaching reading*. Boston, MA: Addison-Wesley Educational Publishers, Inc.

Daniels, H. (2002). *Literature circles: voice and choice in book clubs and reading groups*. Portland, ME: Stenhouse Publishers.

Donovan, M.S., Bradford, J.D., and Pellegrino, J.W. (Eds.). (2000). *How people learn: bridging research and practice*. Washington: National Academies Press.

Farstrup, A.E. (2002, October/November). IRA: Putting reading and teachers first since 1956. *Reading Today, 20 (2)*.

Freeman, M. (1998). *Teaching the youngest writers*. Gainesville, Fl: Maupin House Publishing Inc.

Gewertz, C. (2002, October). Trusting school community linked to student gains. *Education Week*. Retrieved March 4, 2003, from http://www.edweek.com/ew/

Gordon, L.S. (2002). Listening to teachers. *ENC Focus, 9(1)*. Retrieved April 23, 2003, from http://www.enc.org/professional/guide/

Graves, D.H. (1994). *A fresh look at writing*. Portsmouth, NH: Heinemann.

International Reading Association. (1996). *Teachers as readers book groups: exploring your own literacy* [Brochure]. Newark, DE: Gerald Casey.

Irwin, J.M. (2002). *Facilitator's guide.* IRA Literacy Study Groups: Newark, DE: International Reading Association.

Lyons, C.A. & Pinnell, G.S. (2001). *Systems for change in literacy education: a guide to professional development.* Portsmouth, NH: Heinemann.

Murphy, C.U. (1999). *Study groups.* Journal of Staff Development, (20)3. Retrieved April 23, 2003, from http://www.nsdc.org /library/jsd/murphy203.html.

Murphy, C.U. & Lick, D. (2001). Whole faculty study groups, Retrieved May 14, 2003, from http://www.milwaukee.

K12.wi.us/pages/MPS

Ormrod, J.E. (2000). *Educational Psychology.* Upper Saddle River, NJ: Prentice Hall, Inc.

Ownership Associates, Inc. (2001, Winter). *The Ownership Culture Report*, Retrieved June 20, 2003, from http://www/ownershipassociates.com/ocr4.shtm.

Professional development forming a teacher study group, Retrieved January 27, 2003 from www.commtechlab.msu.edu/sites/letsmet/noframes/bigideas/b9/b9/b9u413html

Richardson, J. (2001, August/September). *Learning teams*. Tools for Schools, (2).

Smith Institute (2002). *Study groups with industry*. Retrieved April 22, 2003, from http:/ www.smithinst.ac.uk/projects/study_groups.

About the Authors

Emily Cayuso is an Instructional Coordinator/Reading Specialist in San Antonio, TX. During the past twenty-seven years, she has taught a variety of primary grades and has worked as a Title I Reading Teacher Specialist. She holds a B.S. and an M.Ed.

Carrie Fegan is an elementary education teacher in San Antonio, TX. She has been teaching K-3 for eight years, and has worked with ESOL students. She has traveled extensively and has taught overseas. She holds a B.A. in Elementary Education.

Darlene McAlister is a teacher in San Antonio, TX. She has taught for thirteen years, and has served as a new teacher mentor. She holds a B.S. and an M.S. in Educational Administration.

Perfect for Study Groups...from Maupin House

Building a Writing Community:
A Practical Guide

Marcia S. Freeman

If you want to create a community of K-5 writers who can speak the language of writers, you will love this book. It's filled with classroom-tested techniques and lessons that provide the direct-instruction portion of writing workshop. Practice the techniques with your class, discuss them with your colleagues, then build a teacher's instruction notebook of examples and lessons. 242 pages. MH# 24. $23.95. For elementary teachers.

Constructing Meaning through Kid-Friendly
Comprehension Strategy Instruction

Nancy N. Boyles

By applying the explicit teaching model to comprehension strategy instruction, Dr. Nancy Boyles offers teachers an easy, effective, and innovative approach to improving students' reading comprehension. This resource includes models, teacher-talk, a complete instructional plan, and real-life examples. Lesson plan templates show teachers how to embed comprehension strategy instruction into guided, shared, and independent reading. Includes study group questions and a CD with reproducibles and classroom visuals. MH# 116. 272 pages. $24.95. For teachers of grades 4-8.

Growing Up Writing

Connie Dierking and Sherra Jones

This invaluable resource helps the primary teacher develop an organized writing curriculum based on explicit instruction. Customize the power of writer's workshop for emerging writers with fifty-nine mini-lessons organized to help you teach print operations, foundation skills, print awareness, and writing craft. Work together in your study groups to design more lessons to share! MH# 106. 144 pages. $19.95. For primary teachers.

Creating Readers with Poetry

Nile Stanley

The message in Creating Readers with Poetry is simple and strong: Poetry helps children learn to read! In this innovative resource, Nile Stanley shows you how poetry supports the teaching of reading. He offers mini-lessons, activity poems, and teaching techniques that provide standards-based reading instruction. Includes an audio CD of poetry performances to use as models. Great for generating study-group discussion! MH# 114. 160 pages. $23.95. For teachers of grades K-6.

Teaching the Youngest Writers

Marcia S. Freeman

The ultimate writing-craft book for K-2 teacher study groups! Use this book as the core of your primary writing programs. Explicitly teach the craft skills that good writers use with models for managing the writing process, and clear explanations for expository, descriptive, and personal narrative writing techniques. This resource helps you take your emerging writers from scribbling to writing well-organized, elaborated pieces. 143 pages. MH# 42. $19.95. For primary teachers.

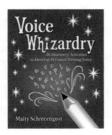

Voice Whizardry

Maity Schrecengost

The thirty-six activities and mini-lessons in this unique resource show you how to release, encourage, and celebrate the personal writing styles of students in grades 3-8. Special Teacher Discoveries help you develop your own writing voice, making this a valuable study group resource for completing professional growth or personal development plans that many districts now require. Suggested literary models and writing samples illustrate voice in both narrative and expository writing. 112 pages. MH# 112. $19.95. For teachers of grades 4-8.